BENIN: HUMAN RIGHTS

EXECUTIVE SUMMARY

Benin is a constitutional democracy. In 2011 President Boni Yayi won a second, and final, five-year term in multi-party elections. In the 2011 legislative elections, President Yayi's supporting coalition, Cowry Force for an Emerging Benin, won 41 of 83 seats in the National Assembly and formed a majority coalition with the Renaissance of Benin Party and other minor supporting parties for a total of 61 seats. As a result, the coalition controlled six of the seven seats in the Bureau of the National Assembly. International observers viewed the presidential and legislative elections as generally free, fair, and transparent. Civilian authorities generally maintained effective control over security forces. Security forces committed some human rights abuses.

The major human rights problems included police use of excessive force; violence and discrimination against women and girls, including female genital mutilation/cutting (FGM/C); and harsh prison conditions.

Other human rights problems included arbitrary arrest and detention and prolonged pretrial detention. Abuse of women and children, including infanticide; trafficking in persons; vigilante violence; and child labor remained problems.

Although the government made an effort to control corruption and abuses, including by prosecuting and punishing public officials, officials sometimes engaged in corrupt practices with impunity.

Section 1. Respect for the Integrity of the Person, Including Freedom from:

a. Arbitrary or Unlawful Deprivation of Life

There were no reports that the government or its agents committed arbitrary or unlawful killings.

In certain instances, elements of security forces shot and killed armed robbers and cited self-defense to explain the shootings. For example, on June 1, policemen chased, shot, and killed in a suburb of Cotonou an individual who highjacked a car in Aplahoue, a village in the southwest region. Security force members stated that the suspect ignored commands to stop. The police issued a report alleging the security force members returned fire in self defense when the suspect shot at them.

b. Disappearance

There were no reports of politically motivated disappearances.

c. Torture and Other Cruel, Inhuman, or Degrading Treatment or Punishment

The constitution and law prohibit such practices, but such incidents occurred. Beatings in custody reportedly were commonplace, according to some suspects who complained of police mistreatment. For example, a March 2012 ruling of the Constitutional Court stated the commissioner of the police station of Houegbo, a village located in the south, violated article 18 of the constitution related to torture and other cruel, inhuman, or degrading treatment or punishment when he instructed his agents to arrest, chain, and severely beat a guard who had a dispute with his supervisor over repayment of a debt.

Prison and Detention Center Conditions

Prison conditions continued to be harsh and life threatening.

Physical Conditions: Overcrowding and lack of proper sanitation and medical facilities posed risks to prisoners' health. A 2010 mediator of the republic (ombudsman) report on conditions in the nine civil prisons stated prisons were overcrowded, with malnutrition and disease common. There were deaths due to lack of ventilation in cramped and overcrowded cells. Lighting was inadequate, but potable tap water was available. Some prisoners suffered from mental illness. There were deaths due to lack of medical care and neglect. Eight of the nine civil prisons were filled far beyond capacity. The 2010 ombudsman's report, commissioned by the president, indicated the total prison population (including pretrial detainees and remand prisoners) was 6,908 in a system with an official capacity of 1,900; of that number, pretrial detainees and remand prisoners totaled 5,174. These numbers did not include police station cells, detention centers, or military lockups. Statistics from 2008 indicated female prisoners were 3.5 percent of the prison population and juveniles were 2.1 percent.

Authorities housed juveniles at times with adults and held pretrial detainees with convicted prisoners, although not with the most violent convicts. On June 5, the president of a parliamentarian opposition group, Union Fait la Nation, summoned the acting minister of justice to discuss trial delays, cell overcrowding, government actions to improve detention conditions, and delayed government publication of the Act on the Penal Procedure Code that was enacted in March.

Administration: Recordkeeping on prisoners was adequate (data on prisoners disaggregated by age, gender, and status were available in prisons). Authorities did not use alternatives to incarceration for nonviolent offenders. The ombudsman visited prisons in Porto-Novo and Parakou in January and February 2012 to examine prison conditions. Authorities allowed prisoners and detainees access to visitors and permitted religious observance. There was no formal system to submit complaints without censorship to judicial authorities, but prisoners could directly address the director of the prison or complain through the normal judicial processes.

Independent Monitoring: The government permitted prison visits by human rights monitors in accordance with their standard modalities. Religious groups and nongovernmental organizations (NGOs) continued to visit prisons, although some NGOs complained credentials were not systematically granted when they submitted requests for visits. On April 9, local NGO Dispensaire Ami des Prisonniers et des Indigents (DAPI-Benin) visited the prison of Abomey in the central region to observe 2013 International Women's Day with female prisoners. Other organizations that visited prisons during the year included the International Committee of the Red Cross, International Federation for Action by Christians for the Abolition of Torture, the local chapter of Prison Fellowship, Caritas, and Prisoners without Borders.

Improvements: In March 2012 the National Assembly passed a new criminal procedure code that had been pending in the National Assembly since 1999. The code aimed to decrease pretrial detention, hasten judicial proceedings, reduce prison congestion, and protect prisoners' rights. The code also established the liberty and detention judge position, to assist courts with better management of arrest warrants, electronic surveillance, and detention. During the year the government completed construction of prisons in the cities of Abomey, Calavi, and Savalou as part of a government-funded project to build10 new prisons. In December 2012 the Cotonou Court of Appeal heard 29 criminal cases involving 57 accused adults. This session was the first since 2009 and was meant to alleviate some prison overcrowding.

d. Arbitrary Arrest or Detention

The constitution and law prohibit arbitrary arrest and detention; however, security forces occasionally failed to observe these prohibitions.

For example, in December 2012 security forces forcibly entered the residence of a businessman on suspicion of his involvement in a robbery the previous day. Security forces held the accused at the Cotonou police station for approximately six hours and then released him after they determined he did not commit the offense. The businessman filed a complaint with the Constitutional Court. The court ruled on August 9 his arrest and detention was arbitrary and in violation of the provisions of the constitution related to arbitrary arrest and requested civil remedies for the violation.

Role of the Police and Security Apparatus

The police, under the Ministry of Interior, have primary responsibility for enforcing law and maintaining order in urban areas; the gendarmerie, under the Ministry of Defense, performs the same function in rural areas.

Military disciplinary councils deal with minor offenses by members of the military services. The councils have no jurisdiction over civilians. Civilian courts deal with serious crimes involving the military. The country has no military tribunal.

There is an internal affairs division of the police, called the Inspector General, which investigates internal police matters.

The police were inadequately equipped and poorly trained, but the government continued to respond to these problems by recruiting more officers, building more stations, and modernizing equipment during the year; however, problems remained, including impunity.

Arrest Procedures and Treatment of Detainees

The constitution requires arrest warrants based on sufficient evidence and issued by a duly authorized official, and requires a hearing before a magistrate within 48 hours, but this was not always observed. Under exceptional circumstances the magistrate may authorize continued detention not to exceed eight days. Detainees have the right to prompt judicial determination, which was generally observed. Detainees were promptly informed of charges against them. They have the right to prompt access to a lawyer after being brought before a judge, which authorities also generally observed. They are allowed to have family visits. After examining a detainee, the judge has 24 hours to decide whether to continue to detain or release the individual. Defendants awaiting judicial decisions may request release on bail; however, the attorney general must agree to the request. Warrants authorizing pretrial detention were effective for six months and could be renewed every six months until a suspect was brought to trial. The government provided counsel to indigents in criminal cases.

There were credible reports gendarmes and police often exceeded the legal limit of 48 hours of detention, sometimes by as much as a week. Authorities often used the practice of holding a person indefinitely "at the disposal of" the Public Prosecutor's Office before presenting the case to a magistrate.

Arbitrary Arrest: The constitution and law prohibit arbitrary arrest, but, at times the authorities did not respect this prohibition.

Pretrial Detention: Approximately 75 percent of persons in prison were pretrial detainees; the length of excess pretrial detentions varied from two to 11 years, according to a mediator's report. Inadequate facilities, poorly trained staff, and overcrowded dockets delayed the administration of justice.

e. Denial of Fair Public Trial

The constitution and law provide for an independent judiciary, but the government did not always respect this provision. The government names judges at the public prosecutor's office, making them susceptible to government influence; however, there were no instances in which the outcome of trials appeared predetermined, and authorities respected court orders. The judicial system was also subject to corruption, although in the past year the government has undertaken substantial anticorruption efforts, including the creation of an independent National Anti-Corruption Authority and the dismissal and arrest of government officials allegedly involved in corruption scandals.

Trial Procedures

While the constitution provides for the right to a fair trial, judicial inefficiency and corruption impeded exercise of this right.

The legal system is based on French civil law and local customary law. A defendant is presumed innocent. Jury trials are used in criminal cases. A defendant has the right to be present at trial and to representation by an attorney.

The court provides indigent defendants with counsel upon request in criminal cases. Government-provided counsel, however, was not always available, especially in cases handled in courts located in the north, because the majority of lawyers lived in the south. A defendant has the right to confront witnesses and to have access to government-held evidence. Defendants are allowed to present witnesses and evidence on their own behalf. Defendants can appeal criminal convictions to the Court of Appeals and the Supreme Court, after which they may appeal to the president for a pardon. Trials are open to the public, but in exceptional circumstances the president of the court may decide to restrict access to preserve public order or to protect the parties. The government extends the above rights to all citizens without discrimination.

Political Prisoners and Detainees

There were no reports of political prisoners or detainees.

Civil Judicial Procedures and Remedies

There is an independent judiciary in civil matters. If administrative or informal remedies are unsuccessful, a citizen may file a complaint concerning an alleged human rights violation with the Constitutional Court. The Constitutional Court's rulings, however, are not binding on courts. An individual can appeal to the Economic Community of West African States' Court of Justice.

f. Arbitrary Interference with Privacy, Family, Home, or Correspondence

The constitution and law prohibit such actions, and the government generally respected these prohibitions. The law requires police to obtain a judicial warrant before entering a private home, and they generally observed this requirement.

Section 2. Respect for Civil Liberties, Including:

a. Freedom of Speech and Press

Although the constitution and law provide for freedom of speech, the government did not always respect this right. There were radio and television broadcasts in which citizens openly criticized the president's policies without reprisal; however, the government occasionally inhibited freedom of the press.

Freedom of Speech: The law provides for prison sentences involving compulsory labor for certain actions related to abuse of the right of free expression. Penalties are for threats to public order or calls to violence.

In September 2012 President Yayi filed a defamation and libel suit against his former legal advisor, who strongly criticized on television the inadequacy of the president's efforts to fight corruption. On January 23, a court sentenced the former legal advisor to six months in prison and a fine of 500,000 CFA francs ($1,031). On January 30, President Yayi granted a pardon to his critic.

Press Freedoms: The independent media were active and expressed a wide variety of views without restriction. Publications criticized the government freely and frequently. A nongovernmental media ethics commission continued to censure some journalists during the year for unethical conduct, such as reporting falsehoods or inaccuracies or releasing information that was under embargo by the government.

The government continued to own and operate the most influential media organizations by controlling broadcast range and infrastructure. The coverage rate for the state-owned television and radio was 96 percent due to powerful transmission equipment owned by the government. Private television and radio had poorer coverage due to inadequate equipment and limited broadcast ranges awarded by the High Authority of Audiovisual and Communication (HAAC).

The majority of citizens were illiterate, lived in rural areas, and generally received their news via radio. The state-owned Office de Radiodiffusion et Television du Benin (ORTB) broadcasts in French and local languages. There were an estimated 78 private, community, and commercial radio stations, two government-owned radio stations, and five private television stations. On July 31, the government created a second state-owned television station, Benin Business 24. Rural community radio stations received support from the ORTB and broadcast several hours a day, exclusively in local languages. Radio France International and the BBC broadcast in Cotonou. The government gave a yearly grant of 350 million CFA ($721,000) in financial assistance to the private media during the year.

Censorship or Content Restrictions: Some journalists practiced self-censorship because they were indebted to government officials who granted them service contracts.

In November 2012 the government, acting through the HAAC, suspended the broadcasting rights of two current events talk shows on a major private television station, citing "lack of balanced opinions" as the cause. Those programs, which had been famous for their strong criticisms of the government, did not return to the air. Some journalists practiced self-censorship because they were afraid of similar government actions to suspend their media outlets or feared being charged by the government with criminal libel. The HAAC publicly warned media outlets against publishing any information related to legal cases currently pending before a criminal court, because it could be interpreted as an attempt to influence the ruling of the court. It was also possible to purchase favorable coverage in the press, thereby influencing content and reporting.

Libel Laws/National Security: The law criminalizes not only libel but also the reprinting or broadcasting of allegedly libelous statements. In December 2012 a court sentenced the director of one of the three largest private television channels to three months in prison for allowing her station to rebroadcast a taped program in which comments critical of the president were made (see above). She was later pardoned by the president. The law prohibits private citizens and the press from declaring or predicting election results.

A private press union leader indicated courts continued to receive libel cases against journalists during the year, but judges generally refrained from prosecuting them. During the year no journalists were prosecuted. Journalists continued to fight for the decriminalization of press-related offenses.

Internet Freedom

There were no government restrictions on access to the internet or credible reports that the government monitored e-mail or internet chat rooms without judicial oversight. According to the International Telecommunication Union, the percentage of individuals using the internet in 2012 was 3.8 percent.

Academic Freedom and Cultural Events

There were no government restrictions on academic freedom or cultural events.

b. Freedom of Peaceful Assembly and Association

The constitution and law provide for freedom of assembly and association. Permits are required for demonstrations and other public gatherings. The government generally respected these rights, although opposition groups cited instances in which they did not seek permits, anticipating they would be opposed-- but there were no instances of actual denial on political grounds (see details below).

Freedom of Assembly

The constitution and law provide for freedom of assembly, and the government generally respected this right.

The government requires permits for use of public places for demonstrations and generally granted such permits. Authorities sometimes cited "public order" to deny requests for permits from opposition groups, civil society organizations, and labor unions. For example, on July 24, police arrested 10 individuals in Abomey-Calavi, a suburb of Cotonou, for organizing a demonstration without government authorization against the president's proposed amendments to the constitution. Police later released all of the individuals without charge.

Freedom of Association

The constitution and law provide for freedom of association, and the government generally respected this right. The government requires associations to register and routinely granted registration.

c. Freedom of Religion

See the Department of State's *International Religious Freedom Report* at www.state.gov/j/drl/irf/rpt.

d. Freedom of Movement, Internally Displaced Persons, Protection of Refugees, and Stateless Persons

The constitution and law provide for freedom of internal movement, foreign travel, emigration, and repatriation, and the government generally respected these rights.

The government cooperated with the Office of the UN High Commissioner for Refugees (UNHCR) and other humanitarian organizations in assisting refugees and asylum seekers. Numbers of internally displaced persons, returning refugees, and registered stateless persons were not significant. Since 2011 the country has been a signatory to the 1954 Convention relating to the Status of Stateless Persons and the 1961 Convention on the Reduction of Statelessness.

On June 20, World Refugee Day, the Ministry of Interior, in conjunction with Benin's UNHCR Office, issued gratis long-term residence permits to 3,558 refugees and asylum seekers, including nationals of Togo, Cote d'Ivoire, Chad, Burundi, Syria, the Central African Republic, and the Democratic Republic of the Congo.

In-Country Movement: The presence of police, gendarmes, and illegal roadblocks impeded domestic movement. Roadblocks were justified as a means of enforcing vehicle safety and customs regulations, but many checkpoints served as a means for police and gendarmes to exact bribes from travelers. The government maintained previously implemented measures to combat such corruption at roadblocks, but they were not always effective, and extortion commonly occurred.

Foreign Travel: The government maintained documentary requirements for minors traveling abroad as part of its continuing campaign against trafficking in persons. This was not always enforced, and trafficking of minors across borders continued.

The government's policy toward the seasonal movement of livestock allowed migratory Fulani (Peul) herdsmen from other countries to enter and depart freely; the government did not enforce designated entry points.

Protection of Refugees

The government has established a system for providing protection to refugees. During the year the government and the UNHCR initiated local integration or repatriation of 3,186 Togolese refugees from the Agame refugee camp and throughout Benin. The government provided protection against the expulsion or return of refugees to countries where their lives or freedom would be threatened on account of their race, religion, nationality, membership in a particular social group, or political opinion. If individuals do not qualify as refugees under the 1951 UN Refugee Convention or the 1967 Protocol, authorities direct them to the immigration office to apply for a residence permit.

Access to Asylum: The law provides for the granting of asylum or refugee status, and the government has established a system for providing protection to refugees.

Employment: The government continued to permit Togolese refugees residing in local communities and refugee camps to participate in most economic activities and enroll their children in local schools.

Durable Solutions: The government and the UNHCR continued to provide assistance to Togolese refugees, and to refugees of other nationalities who integrated into local communities after the closure of the Kpomasse refugee camp. A total of 3,727 refugees of various nationalities enrolled in a joint government and UNHCR program to obtain residency status, housing, and financial assistance for developing income earning activities that facilitate their local integration. Some refugees refused to participate in the program in hopes of repatriation outside of Benin--requests that did not comply with UNHCR regulations. The government also undertook a review of 38 applications by refugees for Beninese citizenship.

Section 3. Respect for Political Rights: The Right of Citizens to Change Their Government

The constitution and law provide citizens the right to change their government peacefully, and citizens exercised this right through periodic, free, and fair elections based on universal suffrage.

Elections and Political Participation

Recent Elections: The country held presidential elections in March 2011 and legislative elections in April 2011. International observers viewed the presidential and legislative elections as generally free and fair. Both elections were hampered by delays on voting days, usually in receiving voting materials or due to polling place staff arriving late. Even with delays, all polling stations remained open the full nine hours required by law. There were no reports of eligible voters unable to cast ballots.

Political Parties: Parties could freely run candidates for election. There were no government restrictions on the political opposition. No single party or group has recently dominated politics. For legislative elections, all candidates must be associated with a political party. T here were no independent candidates.

Participation of Women and Minorities: There were six women among the 83 members in the National Assembly and six female ministers in the 26-member cabinet. The Constitutional Court had two women among its seven justices.

The country has no majority ethnic group. Various ethnic groups were well represented in government agencies, including the civil service and the armed forces. Eight cabinet ministers were from the Bariba, Somba, and Dendi ethnic groups; 12 were from the Fon, Goun, and Adja ethnic groups; and five were from the Yoruba and Nago ethnic groups.

Section 4. Corruption and Lack of Transparency in Government

Although the law provides criminal penalties for official corruption, the government did not implement the law effectively, and officials sometimes engaged in corrupt practices with impunity. The World Bank's most recent Worldwide Governance Indicators reflected that corruption continued to be a serious problem.

Corruption: President Yayi continued his 2006 anticorruption initiative. In August 2011 the National Assembly approved Act 2011-20 on the Fight against Corruption and Related Offenses in the Republic of Benin (Act 2011-20), pending since 2006, to prevent corruption and related offenses. In October 2011 the president signed the act into law.

On July 24, the National Assembly established a fact-finding committee to look into mayors' management of a government funding mechanism (FADEC) for the development of communes, following allegations of mismanagement by certain mayors.

On February 12, President Yayi named 11 members from the public and private sectors to serve on the National Anti-Corruption Authority (ANLC). Yayi appointed the 11 members pursuant to Act 2011-20, which established the ANLC.

The government took a number of actions during the year to combat corruption. The State Audit Office conducted financial audits of several state companies to verify if public funds were well managed.

Based on findings from the state audit office investigation, on May 13, the government fired and arrested the general manager of the oil parastatal Sonacop, who was accused of granting under-the-table contracts, stealing gas for personal use, and conducting business with a company accused of money laundering.

President Yayi continued to fight corruption in port operations. In September 2012 he dismissed the secretary general of the presidency, the director of the port, and the chief of staff of the Ministry of Maritime Economy for allegedly demanding bribes in connection with the construction of a dry port at Tori.

Police corruption was widespread. Police continued to extort money from travelers at roadblocks. For example, in August 2011 authorities caught two police officers regulating traffic at "La Gaite" roundabout in Cotonou extorting money from travelers. Police arrested and jailed the two officers for disciplinary infraction.

On June 27, the Watchdog to Combat Corruption (OLC), a governmental agency, launched the 2011 White Paper on the Perception of Corruption, a nationwide survey which focused on corruption in 11 sectors of the public administration. On June 28, the OLC officially closed and was replaced by the newly staffed ANLC.

It was commonly believed, and acknowledged by some judicial personnel, that the judicial system at all levels was susceptible to corruption. In December 2011 the minister of justice publicly stated judges were corrupt. Judges expressed their disapproval of the minister's statement by going on strike several times during the year.

Whistleblower Protection: The Act 2011-20 provides protection to public and private employees for making internal disclosures or lawful public disclosures of evidence of corrupt practices. There were no reports, however, that the law was implemented effectively to protect whistleblowers.

Financial Disclosure: The law requires income and asset disclosure by appointed and elected public officials. Supreme Court and courts of appeals' chambers of accounts are mandated to monitor and verify disclosures. Declarations are not made available to the public.

Public Access to Information: There are no laws providing for public access to government information, and it was unclear whether requests for such access were granted.

Section 5. Governmental Attitude Regarding International and Nongovernmental Investigation of Alleged Violations of Human Rights

A number of domestic and international human rights groups generally operated without government restriction, investigating and publishing their findings on human rights cases. Government officials often were cooperative and responsive to their views.

UN and Other International Bodies: In 2011 the government cooperated with the UN and other international bodies by providing human rights information to the special rapporteur on the independence of judges and lawyers, the special rapporteur on trafficking in persons, especially in women and children, and the UN High Commissioner's Working Group on Discrimination Against Women.

Government Human Rights Bodies: The government met with domestic NGO monitors through the National Human Rights Advisory Board (CNCDH) and the Ministry of Justice, Legislation, and Human Rights. The ministry donated computers to 11 local NGO members of the CNCDH. The ministry coordinated awareness campaigns to educate the populace on human rights. The ministry's Human Rights Office installed a hotline to allow concerned citizens to alert authorities to suspected human rights violations.

In 2012 the ombudsman visited prisons and documented shortcomings in prison conditions. The ombudsman's report was made public. The ombudsman was independent and adequately resourced.

Section 6. Discrimination, Societal Abuses, and Trafficking in Persons

The constitution and laws prohibit discrimination based on race, gender, disability, language, and social status, but societal discrimination against women continued. Persons with disabilities were disadvantaged. The government took some measures to address these problems but fell short of a comprehensive response.

Women

Rape and Domestic Violence: The law prohibits rape, but enforcement was weak due to police ineffectiveness, official corruption, and victim unwillingness to report cases due to fear of social stigma and retaliation. Although the penal code does not distinguish between rape in general and spousal rape, Act No. 2011-26 of January 9 on the Prevention and Repression of Violence Against Women explicitly prohibits spousal rape and provides the maximum penalty for perpetrators who rape their domestic partners. Prison sentences for rape convictions ranged from one to five years. The new law reinforces existing legislation against gender-based violence. For 2012 the Ministry of Family's Social Promotion Centers recorded a total of 6,368 gender-based violence cases, of which 3,513 involved women, 1,678 involved girls, 555 involved men, and 622 involved boys. Statistics were not available on prosecutions or convictions. Because of the lack of police training in collecting evidence associated with sexual assaults, victim ignorance of the law, and inherent difficulties victims faced in preserving and presenting evidence in court, judges reduced most sexual offenses to misdemeanors.

The penal code prohibits domestic violence, and penalties ranged from six to 36 months' imprisonment. Domestic violence against women was common, however. Women remained reluctant to report cases. Judges and police were reluctant to intervene in domestic disputes, which is how society generally viewed such cases. The local chapter of the regional NGO Women in Law and Development-Benin, the Female Jurists Association of Benin, and the Action Group for Justice and Social Equality offered social, legal, medical, and psychological assistance to victims of domestic violence. The Office of Women's Promotion under the jurisdiction of the Ministry of Family and Solidarity is responsible for protecting and advancing women's rights and welfare.

Female Genital Mutilation/Cutting (FGM/C): (see section 6, Children).

Sexual Harassment: The law prohibits sexual harassment and offers protection for victims. Under the law persons convicted of sexual harassment face sentences of one to two years in prison and fines ranging from 100,000 to one million CFA ($206 to $2,060). The law also provides penalties for persons who are aware of sexual harassment and do not report it. Enforcement of these laws was lax due to law enforcement agents' and prosecutors' lack of legal knowledge and necessary skills to pursue such cases and victims' fear of social stigma and retaliation. Although this specific law was not widely enforced, judges used other provisions in the penal code to deal with sexual abuses involving minors. Sexual harassment was common, especially of female students by their male teachers.

Reproductive Rights: The constitution provides that the government should protect the family, particularly the mother and the child. The law promotes responsible fertility to reduce early and/or late childbearing and promotes family planning through the distribution of contraceptives. The law guarantees couples' and individuals' reproductive rights, including access to health care, freedom to give birth, freedom of marriage, rights to nondiscrimination, access to contraception, and equal access to health care for people living with sexually transmitted infections, including HIV. The law provides penalties for the commission of all acts prejudicial to the enjoyment of sexual and reproductive health. The government generally respected these rights. An estimated 30 percent of women had an unmet need for family planning. According to data from the 2012 Benin Multiple Indicator Demographic and Health Survey, just 8 percent of women and girls ages 15-49 used a modern method of contraception. In 2011 a total of 84 percent of births were attended by skilled health personnel. According to WHO, the maternal mortality rate was 350 deaths per 100,000 live births in 2010; factors contributing to the high rate were deliveries without adequate medical assistance, lack of access to emergency obstetric care, and unhygienic conditions during birth.

Discrimination: Although the constitution provides for equality for women in the political, economic, and social spheres, women experienced extensive discrimination because of societal attitudes and resistance to behavioral change. Women experienced discrimination in obtaining employment, credit, equal pay, and in owning or managing businesses.

The code of persons and the family bans all discrimination against women regarding marriage and provides for the right to equal inheritance. The nationality law, however, discriminates against women. According to Act No. 65-17, the child of a Beninese father is automatically considered a Beninese citizen, but the child of a Beninese woman is considered Beninese only if the child's father is unknown, has no known nationality, or is also Beninese.

In rural areas women traditionally occupy a subordinate role and are responsible for much of the hard labor on subsistence farms. In urban areas women dominated the informal trading sector in the open-air markets. During the year the government and NGOs continued to educate the public on the sections of law that provide women with inheritance and property rights and significantly increase their rights in marriage, including prohibitions on forced marriage, child marriage, and polygamy.

During the year the government continued to grant microcredit to poor persons, especially to women in rural areas, to help them develop income-generating activities. The government extended credit and loans to female entrepreneurs. From 2007-12, 95 percent of the approximately 1.8 million persons identified as most needy were women.

Children

The Ministry of Family is responsible for the protection of children's rights, primarily in the areas of education and health. The National Commission for Children's Rights and the Ministry of Family have oversight of the promotion of human rights with regard to child welfare.

Birth Registration: Citizenship is derived by birth within the country and/or from the father. Particularly in rural areas, parents often did not declare the birth of their children, either out of ignorance or because they could not afford the fees for birth certificates. This could result in denial of public services such as education and health care. The government, through an Administrative Census for Birth Registration, issued birth certificates to children who did not have one. Several donors operated programs to increase the number of registered children. For example, UNICEF continued to support the government's campaign to register every birth and provide birth certificates to those who did not have the chance to get one when they were born. The Ministry of Interior, with donors' assistance, hosted a national forum in July 2012 in Cotonou to discuss ways to improve the civil registration system.

Education: Primary education was compulsory for all children between six and 11 years of age. Education became tuition-free for all children starting with the 2007-08 school year, but parents often voluntarily paid tuition for their children because many schools had insufficient funds. Girls did not have the same educational opportunities as boys, and female literacy was approximately 18 percent, compared with 50 percent male literacy. In some parts of the country, girls received no formal education. According to UNICEF, the net primary school enrollment rate in 2007 was approximately 93 percent for boys and 83 percent for girls. The enrollment rate for secondary education was much lower for girls.

Child Abuse: Children underwent multiple forms of abuse including rape, sexual harassment, abduction, and debauchery/defilement. The Central Office for Minors Protection in Cotonou arrested suspects and referred them to court.

Forced and Early Marriage: The law prohibits marriage under age 18 but allows underage marriage (14 to 17) with parental consent, the consent of the underage individuals, and authorization of a judge. The last 2012 UN Population Fund (UNFPA) update of the percentage of women ages 20-24 years married before age 18 in Benin was 34.4 percent. Child marriage included forced marriage, barter marriage, and marriage by abduction. A 2008 gender-based violence survey conducted in 13 communes indicated 23 percent of the 594 children interviewed were subjected to forced and precocious marriage. As part of forced marriage, there is a tradition in which a groom abducts and rapes his prospective child bride. The practice was widespread in rural areas, despite government and NGO efforts to end it through information sessions on the rights of women and children. Local NGOs reported some communities concealed the practice.

Harmful Traditional Practices: Female genital mutilation/cutting (FGM/C) was practiced on girls and women from infancy up to age 30, although the majority of cases occurred before age 13, with half occurring before age five. The type of FGM/C most commonly perpetrated was Type II, the total removal of the clitoris with or without the total excision of the labia minora. This practice was largely limited to remote rural areas in the north. The law prohibits FGM/C and provides penalties for performing the procedure, including prison sentences of up to 10 years and fines of up to six million CFA ($12,360); however, enforcement was rare due to the code of silence associated with this crime. Individuals who were aware of an incident of FGM/C but did not report it potentially faced fines ranging from 50,000 to 100,000 CFA ($103 to $206). Approximately 13 percent of women and girls have been subjected to FGM/C; the figure was higher in some regions, especially the northern departments, including Alibori and Donga (48 percent) and Borgou (59 percent), and among certain ethnic groups. More than 70 percent of Bariba and Peul (Fulani) and 53 percent of Yoa-Lokpa women and girls had undergone FGM/C. Younger women were less likely to be excised than their older counterparts. Those who performed the procedure, usually older women, profited from it.

NGOs continued to educate rural communities about the dangers of FGM/C and to retrain FGM/C practitioners in other activities. The government, in conjunction with NGOs and international partners, made progress in raising public awareness of the danger of the practice. The Ministry of Family continued an education campaign that included conferences in schools and villages, discussions with religious and traditional authorities, and display of educational banners. NGOs also addressed this problem in local languages on local radio stations. On June 18, the country's traditional rulers issued a public statement expressing commitment to reducing traditional practices harmful to boys' and girls' health.

Sexual Exploitation of Children: The penal code provides penalties for rape, sexual exploitation, corruption of minors, and procuring and facilitating prostitution, and it increases penalties for cases involving children under 15 years old. The child trafficking law provides penalties for all forms of child trafficking, including child prostitution. Under the penal code, individuals involved in child prostitution, including those who facilitate and solicit it, face imprisonment of two to five years and fines of 1,000,000 to 10,000,000 CFA ($2,060 to $20,600). The law does not specifically prohibit child pornography. The de facto minimum age for consensual sex is 18.

Child prostitution continued in some areas. Some children, including street children, engaged in prostitution to support themselves without the involvement of an adult. The penal code prohibits child prostitution; however, enforcement was limited, and the commercial sexual exploitation of children occurred. Cases of child sex tourism, involving both boys and girls, were reported in the Department of Mono and on the shores of the Bight of Benin. A 2009 report on the commercial sexual exploitation of children in 11 communes indicated that 43.2 percent of surveyed children (ages 12-17) who engaged in prostitution were also subjected to commercial sexual exploitation.

Through the traditional practice of vidomegon, which literally means "placed child," poor, generally rural, children are placed in the home of a wealthier family for educational or vocational opportunities and a higher standard of living. In many cases, however, they are not afforded these opportunities, and although the child receives living accommodations, she or he often faces long hours of work, inadequate food, and sexual exploitation – factors indicative of forced labor and exploitation of children in domestic servitude. Sometimes the income generated by the child's activities is split between the child's parents and the urban family that raises the child. Up to 95 percent of children in vidomegon were young girls. Several local NGOs led public education and awareness campaigns to decrease the practice.

Criminal courts meted out stiff sentences to criminals convicted of crimes against children, but many such cases never reached the courts due to lack of awareness about the law and children's rights, lack of access to courts, or fear of police involvement.

Infanticide or Infanticide of Children with Disabilities: Despite widespread NGO campaigns, the traditional practices of killing deformed babies, breech babies, babies whose mothers died in childbirth, and one of two newborn twins (because they were considered sorcerers) continued in the north. In March 2012 the ombudsman held a national forum on ritual infanticide in Parakou.

International Child Abductions: The country is not a party to the 1980 Hague Convention on the Civil Aspects of International Child Abduction.

Anti-Semitism

There was no known Jewish community, and there were no reports of anti-Semitic acts.

Trafficking in Persons

See the Department of State's *Trafficking in Persons Report* at www.state.gov/j/tip.

Persons with Disabilities

The law does not explicitly prohibit discrimination against persons with physical, sensory, intellectual, or mental disabilities in education, access to health care, or provision of other state services; however, the law provides that the government should care for persons with disabilities. There were no legal requirements for the construction or alteration of buildings to permit access for persons with disabilities. Legislation is general in nature and addresses equality, equity, and nondiscrimination among all citizens. Several laws, however, including the labor code, the social security code, the Persons and Family Code, and the 2011 law establishing general rules for elections contain specific references to persons with disabilities. The country also has a National Policy for the Protection and Integration of Persons with Disabilities. Children with mental, visual, and physical disabilities, however, continued to suffer social exclusion and had no access to the conventional educational system.

The government operated few institutions to assist persons with disabilities. The Office for the Rehabilitation and the Insertion of Persons with Disabilities under the jurisdiction of the Ministry of Family coordinated assistance to persons with disabilities through the Aid Fund for the Rehabilitation and Insertion of Persons with Disabilities (Fonds Ariph).

The labor code includes provisions to protect the rights of workers with disabilities, which were enforced with limited effectiveness during the year.

In 2011 a blind woman filed an appeal with the Constitutional Court to complain about the Ministry of Labor and Civil Service's rejection of her application to sit for a competitive exam to recruit young magistrates. The ministry claimed it was not equipped to offer the exam in Braille. The Constitutional Court stated in May 2012 the decision of the Ministry of Labor and Civil Service discriminated against the woman. Rulings by the Constitutional Court, however, are not binding.

The Office of Labor under the Ministry of Labor and Civil Service and the Ministry of Family are responsible for protecting the rights of persons with disabilities.

Societal Abuses, Discrimination, and Acts of Violence Based on Sexual Orientation and Gender Identity

There are no laws explicitly criminalizing consensual same-sex sexual activity. There are laws prohibiting discrimination against other groups but none that specifically reference lesbian, gay, bisexual, and transgender (LGBT) individuals. There were no reports of criminal or civil cases involving consensual same-sex conduct or reports of societal discrimination or violence based on a person's sexual orientation. Although homosexual behavior was socially discouraged, it was neither prosecuted nor persecuted. A growing number of citizens were open about their sexual orientation or gender identity, but the LGBT community remained largely disorganized and hidden.

Other Societal Violence or Discrimination

There were no reports of discrimination or violence based on HIV/AIDS status. It is illegal to discriminate against persons, at any stage of hiring or employment, based on such status.

Police generally ignored vigilante attacks, and incidents of mob violence continued to occur, in part due to the perceived failure of local courts to punish criminals adequately. Such cases generally involved mobs killing or severely injuring suspected criminals, particularly thieves caught stealing. For instance, on April 30, local residents of Doko-Agbongnizounhoue, in the commune of Toviklin, intercepted a man and a woman who were suspected of stealing a motorbike. The crowd beat and burned the two suspects to death. The police reportedly did not investigate the killing or arrest the perpetrators.

Killing to obtain human body parts for ritual purposes occurred. Both adults and children were victims.

Section 7. Worker Rights

a. Freedom of Association and the Right to Collective Bargaining

The labor code allows workers, including government employees, to form and join independent unions of their choice without previous authorization or excessive requirements. New unions must register with the Ministry of Interior, a three-month process, or risk a fine.

The law also protects the right to strike. Workers, including civil servants and employees of private and public companies, including parastatals, have the right to strike.

The merchant marine code grants seafarers the right to organize, but they do not have the right to strike.

The law provides that civil servants, public and private entity workers, and parastatal employees who provide essential services shall maintain minimum services during strikes. The act states that essential services refer to services pertaining to health, security, energy, water, air transport, and telecommunications. Workers must provide three days' notice before striking. Authorities can declare strikes illegal for reasons such as threatening social peace and order and can requisition striking workers to maintain minimum services. The government may prohibit any strike on the grounds it threatens the economy or the national interest. Laws prohibit employer retaliation against strikers, except that a company may withhold part of a worker's pay following a strike.

There are no restrictions on collective bargaining. The labor code provides for collective bargaining, and workers freely exercised this right with the exception of merchant shipping employees. The government sets wages in the public sector by law and regulation. Workers discussed labor-related issues with employers through the National Consultation and Collective Bargaining Commission.

The law allows unions to conduct their activities without interference, prohibits antiunion discrimination, and provides for reinstatement of workers fired for union activity. Employers may not take union membership or activity into account in hiring, work distribution, professional or vocational training, or dismissal.

While the government generally respected the right to form and join independent unions, and workers, including civil servants, exercised the right to strike, the government did not effectively enforce these laws, particularly in the informal sector. The government did not enforce the provisions on antiunion discrimination and reinstatement. Information regarding whether or not remedies and penalties had deterrent effects was not available.

Freedom of association and the right to collective bargaining were generally respected. Worker organizations are independent of the government and political parties. Civil servants went on strike throughout the year. There were reports, however, that employers threatened individuals with dismissal for union activity.

The National Consultation and Collective Bargaining Commission held sessions and met with the government during the year to discuss workers' claims and propose solutions.

On May 31, the country's confederation of trade unions issued a public statement charging the government with human rights violations, restriction of freedom of speech and movement, and intimidation of union leaders. It accused the government of authorizing public demonstrations and gatherings of government supporters, while preventing groups from demonstrating against the government.

No violations related to collective bargaining rights were reported.

b. Prohibition of Forced or Compulsory Labor

The labor code does not prohibit all forms of forced or compulsory labor, including by children, and provides for imprisonment with compulsory labor. The law allows authorities to exact work from military conscripts which is not limited to work of a purely military character. The laws regulating various acts or activities relating to the exercise of freedom of expression allow imposition of prison sentences involving obligation to perform social rehabilitation work.

Forced labor occurred, including mainly domestic servitude and bonded labor by children. Forced labor was mainly found in the agricultural (e.g., cotton and palm oil), artisanal mining, quarrying, fishing, commercial, and construction sectors. Many traffickers were relatives or acquaintances of their victims, exploiting the traditional system of vidomegon, in which parents allow their children to live with and work for richer relatives, usually in urban areas (see section 6).

Also see the Department of State's *Trafficking in Persons Report* at www.state.gov/j/tip.

c. Prohibition of Child Labor and Minimum Age for Employment

The labor code prohibits the employment or apprenticeship of children under age 14 in any enterprise; however, children between ages 12 and 14 may perform domestic work and temporary or seasonal light work if it does not interfere with their compulsory schooling. The code bans night work for young workers under 18 unless special dispensation is allowed by the government in consultation with the National Labor Council. Young workers under age18 are entitled to a minimum 12-hour consecutive break including the nighttime period. The law lists hazardous work activities that are prohibited for children under 18 and includes 22 trades and 74 related hazardous activities.

The laws were not effectively enforced. The Labor Office, under the Ministry of Labor and Civil Service, enforced the labor code only in the formal sector due to a lack of inspectors. There were 75 labor officers, comprised of 56 labor inspectors, 15 administrators, and four labor controllers. The 56 inspectors lacked the means to fully implement necessary inspections. The total number of inspections conducted during the year was unavailable. Penalties for violating the laws were sufficiently strict to serve as a deterrent. The labor code provides fines ranging from 140,000 CFA ($296) to 350,000 CFA ($722) and/or sentences of two months to one year in prison for individuals involved in forced labor.

Despite the government's limited capacity to enforce child labor laws, the government did continue to take steps to educate parents on the labor code and prevent compulsory labor by children, including through media campaigns, regional workshops, and public pronouncements on child labor problems. These initiatives were part of the Labor Office's traditional sensitization program. The government also worked with a network of NGOs and journalists to educate the population about child labor and child trafficking.

In July 2012 the government approved the National Action Plan for the Elimination of the Worst Forms of Child Labor. On July 12, the Ministry of Labor and Civil Service, in conjunction with an international donor, led a kick-off event for the national action plan.

In 2011 the government signed an accord with the Republic of the Congo aimed at halting the trafficking of children between the two countries. In February 2012 the government hosted a three-day workshop to draft and approve a joint action plan to fight child trafficking in Benin and the Congo. On August 17, Beninese authorities, in conjunction with their Congolese counterparts, facilitated the repatriation of 10 Beninese victims of child trafficking from the Congo and Gabon.

Child labor remained a problem due in part to limited government capacity to enforce the law. To help support their families, children of both sexes--including those as young as seven – continued to work on family farms, in small businesses, on construction sites in urban areas, in public markets as street vendors, and as domestic servants under the practice of vidomegon. Under the traditional system of vidomegon, many rural parents sent their children to cities to live with relatives or family friends to perform domestic chores in return for receiving an education. Host families did not always honor their part of the arrangement, and abuse and forced labor of child domestic servants was a problem. A majority of children working as apprentices were under the legal age for apprenticeship of 14, including children working in construction, car and motorbike repair, hairdressing, and dressmaking. Children worked as laborers with adults in quarries in many areas. Children were at times forced to hawk goods and beg, and street children engaged in prostitution (see section 6). Children under age 14 worked in either the formal or informal sectors in the following activities: agriculture, hunting and fishing, industry, construction and public works, trade and vending, food and beverages, transportation, and other services, including employment as household staff.

Some parents indentured their children to "agents" recruiting farm hands or domestic workers, often on the understanding the children's wages would be sent to the parents. In some cases these agents took the children to neighboring countries, including Nigeria, Cote d'Ivoire, Togo, and Ghana, for labor.

Also see the Department of State's *Trafficking in Persons Report* at www.state.gov/j/tip and the Department of Labor's *Findings on the Worst Forms of Child Labor* at www.dol.gov/ilab/programs/ocft/tda.htm.

d. Acceptable Conditions of Work

The government set minimum wage scales for a number of occupations. The minimum wage was 30,000 CFA ($62) per month.

The labor code establishes a workweek of between 40 and 46 hours, depending on the type of work, and provides for at least one 24-hour rest period per week. Domestic and agricultural workers frequently worked 70 hours or more per week, above the maximum provided for under the labor code of 12 hours per day or 60 hours per week. The labor code also mandates premium pay for overtime and prohibits excessive compulsory overtime.

The law establishes occupational health and safety standards (OSH). The law does not provide workers with the right to remove themselves from dangerous work situations without jeopardy to continued employment. The government has the authority to require employers to remedy dangerous work conditions but did not effectively do so. Provisions of the law related to acceptable conditions of work apply to all workers. The law also regulates movement of foreigners and requires special authorization for foreigners to leave their town of residence; however, the law was not applied. Significant parts of the work force and foreign workers do not benefit, in practice, from minimum wage scales.

The Ministry of Labor and Civil Service was responsible for enforcement of the minimum wage, workweek, and OSH standards. The ministry did not effectively enforce these standards, however. The authorities generally enforced legal limits on workweeks in the formal sector, but did not effectively monitor or control foreign or migrant workers' conditions of work. Government efforts were impeded by the small number of labor inspectors. Resources were limited. Random inspections were conducted during the year. Penalties for violating the labor code were not sufficient to deter violations. The government took unsuccessful measures to deter people from engaging in the sale of smuggled gas from Nigeria. The government supported informal workers by granting them credits to expand their businesses as part of its microcredit project for the poor.

Many workers had to supplement their wages by subsistence farming or informal sector trade. Most workers in the wage sector earned more than the minimum wage; many domestics and other laborers in the informal sector earned less. Violations of OSH standards mostly occurred in informal sector trades including hairdressing, dressmaking, baking, mechanics, and carpentry, where workers faced biological, chemical, physical, and psychological risks. Children involved in these trades as apprentices worked long hours and were more vulnerable to hazardous working conditions. In some of the mechanic and carpentry shops, children worked alongside adults while the adults used various tools and equipment, and some adults and children lacked adequate protective gear (head, eye, or ear protection, face masks, heavy boots, etc.). According to various sources, informal workers accounted for over 90 percent of the total number of workers in the country. Informal workers faced numerous challenges and vulnerabilities, including long working hours and no social security coverage. They often endured substandard working conditions and were exposed to occupational risks. No data on workplace fatalities and accidents were available.

www.ingramcontent.com/pod-product-compliance
Lightning Source LLC
Chambersburg PA
CBHW080803290526
45790CB00008B/3567